karen t brown

elsewhere

selected poems

Karen

X .

Pittenween

2003

bluebell

first published in great britain 2003
by bluebell 33 limited
9 ikona court, st georges avenue
weybridge surrey kt13 0dw

printed in england

a CIP catalogue record for this book
Is available from the british library.

ISBN 0-9545699-0-3

first edition

www.bluebell33.com

elsewhere

poems by karen t brown

illustrations by jo macfarlane

edited by tim clark

bluebell

about bluebell 33

bluebell 33 is a new publishing business set up in may 2003
to enable people to share, experience and appreciate the
artistic and creative talents of jo macfarlane, an artist who
is originally from pittenweem, in fife, and karen brown,
a writer who is originally from scone, in perthshire.

bluebell 33 is committed to **capturing the essence of
emotions and feelings through illustration and verse**™.
using a variety of media and design techniques we will
enable people to recognise emotions in complementary,
expressive and thought provoking images and words.

for further information please contact us on email at
info@bluebell33.com or visit the website, www.bluebell33.com.

about the author

karen brown was born on 21st july 1970. her poems have been published in a variety of poetry anthologies including 'expressions of a century', a remarkable collection of work offering a poetic approach on the events of the last 100 years, and 'immortal thoughts', a unique and inspirational book of verse, providing an insight into today's modern world. karen has also been commissioned to provide poems for wedding invitations, christenings and christmas cards.

'elsewhere' is her first collected works from which her poems and verse have been used to provide the inspiration for greeting cards designed and published by bluebell 33, a company of which she is one of the three founding directors.

karen developed her passion for literature and the arts at drama school where she was inspired by the works of shakespeare and his ability to paint beautiful pictures of love and pain and robert browning's innate ability to capture characters within his poems. it is now time for karen to share her thought provoking, emotive and lucid style with the world.

contents

inspired by love 27

forest thoughts 49

seasons of change   61

acknowledgements

for as long as I can remember poetry has always been a part
of my life. writing poetry was a normal thing for me growing up
thanks to the creativity and imagination of my mother and the honest
simple words of my father. they understood my need to write, and
saw how much I enjoyed placing words on paper. thank you mum
and dad for bringing out the poet in me, and reading every word I
have ever written.

also my brother, richard, even though we spent much of our young
adult life apart, the lessons I have learned from you are like a
lifetime of teachings.... thank you, for silently being there, and
understanding. you are a wonderful father, and I look forward to
hearing the memories your son will share one day, for you
placed them in his heart.

and for joanna, you were always just a call away, no matter where
in the world we were. I never had to ask for your love and
friendship, you were just always there. I look forward to sharing
our future together. you light up the darkness, and show me
the way....thank you.

and finally tim, you gave me something I only ever wrote about,
a love that has washed away any doubt and pain that I had in my
heart. you saw light in my soul and made me shine. you just
knew I would find my way, and stood beside me, giving the solace
I needed. you know the poems dedicated to you, your smile is
in every word.

foreword

the poems in this book are honest and raw. inspired, not only, by my experiences but more importantly the experiences of people who entered my life, and by the memory of the ones who sadly left.

I dedicate this book to anyone who has ever loved and lost, and to those who have yet to walk towards fates waiting hand.

if you find just one line in this book, and it touches your heart......then I am honoured.

to the memory of my grandfather
gordon wolsey gillies

emoceans

standing by the shore

The ripples on the ocean are kissed by the
Golden summer sun,
Reflecting the cascading waves, as along the
Shore they run.
And with it brings the peaceful echoes of
Promising joyful dreams,
Standing in the bright sunlight, forever, or
So it seems.
For timeless is the ocean, even though it
Sounds a rhythmic beat
Of every heart that looks upon, as the land
And ocean meet.

Then as our lives go on changing, the ocean
Shall always be there,
And when I feel the dream slip away
I will forever stop and stare.
Taking time to recall the memories, when
The sands were of purest gold.
And I imagine myself walking upon them
Allowing those memories to unfold.
Even though we are far away now, in my
Mind I am by the shore
And fondly remember a time we
Shared, the time when it was just us four.

waving goodbye

Like the sand in the shallow waters, I am
Mixed up by emotional waves.
And like the dying sea life, to go back is
All I crave.
Washed up like an empty seashell, a vestige
Of an unfeeling sea,
All I long for is to float slowly backwards
To a place I yearn to be.
Reach out just a little further, caress me
With your ice-cold hands,
For I await your tidal love, that appears
Only when you command.

The ocean crashes against the rocks in a
Defiant roaring cry,
Then slips slowly back from the shoreline
Echoing softly my lonely sigh.
Let the seasons come and go now, all I
Feel is the cascading rain,
For it falls like the tears in my heart
As it waters my growing pain.
But how could you see my emotions, when you
Stand so far from the shore?
If only you had stepped on the beach and
Seen how I could have adored.

So when the land and water meet, on
Time, each and every day,
I will sail out on the horizon, and
Hear only echoes of what you say.

thank you I

For guiding me through an
Ocean of doubt,
And stopping the waves
Washing my dreams away.
For holding me above the water.
And setting sail to the words
That say,
'never turn from the horizon
Use the waves as your
Guiding hand.
Return only when you have
Found them,
And then step safely upon
The sands.'

thank you 2

For stopping me from falling through
A confused sky,
Catching me so softly, when I joined
The clouds to cry.
For taking all those rain drops,
And placing them on the sea.
So when the tide comes in each
Night, my tears are now set free.

the calling shores

As you walk along the cliff path
Feel the wind beneath your wings,
Let your breath be taken away
And join the calling echoes to sing.

Feel your soul reach out to
The ocean, and soar among the birds,
Diving into the deep blue sea then
Rising to be heard.

For your song is so lamenting the
World can hear your cries,
Resting on the rain drops, as it
Falls slowly from the sky.

So no matter where I am, and
I see the falling rain.
I shall be standing on the
Cliff path, ready to ease your
Lonely pain.

midnight sea

The sea is calm tonight, as it
Caresses the midnight shore,
Lit it up by a bright full moon
As across the sky it soars.
And in a cloudless heaven the
Stars reflect upon the sea,
Mirrored in the ripples
As the ocean sets them free.

you are not here

I walk along a breathless shore
For the haunting wind calls your
Name, no more.
I listen through the silence, for the
Slightest sound.
But the echoes have stopped, my ears
Are bound.

Tender whispers that once called my
Name.
Have set like the sun, and put out
The flame.
For the deep ocean has risen too high,
And turned out the light, and
Darkened the sky.

Twilight is here, arriving on time,
But you are not here, you are not mine.
So what use are the stars to me now.
When my heart is broken, my head is bowed.

I do not wish to see the setting sun.
The stars, the moon have all, but gone.
The crashing waves no longer sigh,
Only remind me now of the tears I cry.

So take this loneliness, put it to sail,
For the pain I have shall never fail.
Send it to the horizon, by the setting sun.
So I know where it is, if I ever return.

seashells

I long to hear your laughter
As the waves chase you up the shore,
And see you dancing on the golden
Sands, as the sun shines forever more.
Listening to the shells
As you hear the whispering sea.
Knowing you are loved, as only you can be.

I watch you sleep

I watch you sleep, peaceful
In your dreams.
And I imagine where you are,
Enclosed within those scenes.
Sailing on the ocean,
Rocked gently by the waves.
Lying upon a sun drenched
Deck, restful in the rays.
Breathing in the ocean air,
Captured in the breeze.
Drifting to the horizon,
Above a tranquil sea.

I heard you

I walked towards the sand dunes,
And stood there by your side.
For I had heard you calling
And came to be your guide.

fragile shores

Broken are the promises,
That lie on fragile shores.
Swept up by an angry tide,
Grasping forever more.
No longer can the calm sea,
Hold my dreams alive,
For they sink into the depths
Of the ocean, then dive
Into a watery darkness,
Submerged within those dreams,
The ones I watch drift slowly
Away, silent and unseen.

stop the silence

Controlled by your heart,
Ruled by your mind.
Bid farewell to them both,
And helplessly find.
To plan a journey of love,
Just cannot be.
No boundaries for the wind,
No edges to the sea.

Stand by the ocean, turn your
Back to the waves.
Let the wind take your breath
Let your heart become brave.
Listen as the past takes your hand
Like the whispering shells,
Left on the sand.

For each one holds a memory
That can lie on the shore.
For if you know where it is,
And you are ever unsure.
You can place each one on
The knowing sands.
So when the tide comes in,
They slip from your hands.

Leave the past and only
Return to the distant shore.
For you shall meet yourself,
Like the times before.
Walk to the sand dunes, to
The rising sun.
Do not leave the past, but
See how your life has begun.

pebbles

I stare into the ocean pebbled
With ghosts of the past.
Stretching out on a sand of memories
Motionless where they were cast.

for you

If I took a piece of heaven,
And placed it on the shore.
It would pale in comparison,
To the way that I adore.

For you have come to awaken
Such love within my soul,
And as we walk together
My love for you still grows.

When I stand by the ocean,
I feel you take my hand.
Then together watch the sunset
Upon this tranquil land.

Calming like the ocean,
You stilled the crashing waves,
And hushed the doubting
Echoes that came into the bay.

Now I have a love, that is
Always in my reach.
You and I hand in hand,
Walking slowly on our beach.

footprints

I walk along the shoreline,
But my footsteps fade away.
How will you know to follow
When the path never seems to stay?
But when I look beyond me I
See footprints in the sand,
And then I come to realise you
Were waiting, to take my hand.

falling sun

I sailed out to the horizon,
And left you far behind.
Never allowing my head to turn,
Chasing the memories from my mind.
And like the ebbing sea
My timely journey had begun.
My destiny was the shoreline,
To chase the falling sun.

For when I looked upon you,
No ocean could come between.
Your love had touched my drowning heart,
And risen from my dreams.

skimming stones

Sacred are the tears that,
Fall down from the sky.
Rippling in the pools of doubt,
As the rivers pass me by.
Caught up in a dragging current,
My heart and mind are one the same.
No more skimming on the water,
No more sinking doubts of pain.

casting pebbles

I saw
You by
The shoreline
Casting
Pebbles to
The sea.
Skimming
On the
Ocean,
Recalling
A place
You long
To be.

seahorses

Riding on the waves,
Across a sea of dreams.
Chasing the dancing moonlight,
As it ripples in between.
For galloping to the shoreline,
The waves make their last command.
And return, slowly backwards,
Bidding farewell to the calling sands.

angels of the sea

I hear the calling echoes,
That reach me by the shore.
Brought to me like angels wings,
As across the waves they soar.
Sometimes it sounds like laughter
That joins a lamenting song.
Then a sudden silence as the
Chasing echoes have now gone.
I look up to the night sky,
Resting a moon like a coin of gold,
That lights up the travelling waves,
As the image takes it hold.
For on the dancing water
A beauty swims to me,
And in that rhythmic motion,
I saw the angels of the sea.

inspired by love

the castle wedding

The setting sun falls on the castle walls,
As borthwick stands in glory.
Twilight's hour whispers to twin towers,
And the echoes retell the story.
For you and I know of tales long ago,
And the history these walls must have seen.
The castle stands alone immortalised in stone,
To become a sanctuary for scotland's queen.
As our ancestors call, again the sun falls,
Let us share our future glory,
With love that is long and towered with song,
We shall be part of borthwick's story.

angels wings

Come to me in the darkness of the night.
Come to me my love, in solitude dreams.
Let me dance wildly in your rays of light,
So, your laughter drowns out my lonely screams.
Take my soul on a journey far from here,
And leave my body behind as it sleeps,
Then I shall know, that you are always near,
To wipe away tears my heart softly weeps.
But they shall never fall unseen by you,
As you carefully hold them in your palm.
Then placing them down like the morning dew,
Making the sun reflect upon the calm.
I knew you were mine when I heard you sing,
And you held me tightly in your angel's wings.

the beginning

May the flowers always open
When they know that you walk by.
May the rain come down in clear drops
When the clouds can hear you cry.
Let the sun shine down upon you,
And show you magical things.
For the world shall hear your laughter,
As it awakens the birds to sing.
But this has been wish for you
Right from the very start.
For you were gifted with two people
Who shared their loving hearts.

I miss you

Stop the clock, if I have no time
With you.
For wasted are the days that
I do not share.
What use is time and how can
It be true?
And to the breathing seconds
I have no care.
A useless hourglass shall stand
Unturned.
No use for those meaningless
Sands.
And to the candles that
Nightly burn,
For the falling wax reminds me
Of times cruel hand.

I know

You carried me, when I
Tired of walking alone,
Holding me so tightly,
Until my fears had flown.
You knew when to place me down,
So I could begin once more,
Sheltering me from pain
As the sky begins to pour.
For, knowing you are there,
The sun forever shines,
And I shall walk on always
With your hand in mine.

your dream

Know that I love you,
For I am here,
Even in the darkest night.
Feel my arms around you
When you fear to walk alone,
And when you tire of
Holding your dreams,
Rest them upon me, so I can
Hold them till you awake.

the sunlight

Who will take this great love,
With no fear,
And walk along beside me,
And catch the falling tears?
Who will rest upon me, and
Share their golden dreams
So I can stand inside the sunlight,
Forever in those beams.
For even though I question, I know
The answer now,
And to your kindly love I
Shall duly bow.

without you

Without you, there would be no day.
For the sun would rise unseen and
Set so far away.
No moon would light the midnight sky.
No hands to catch the tears I cry.
But now I stand in the summer sun,
And my fears have all but gone.
For you have placed my dreams before your own
And given me a love that I have never known.

timeless emotion

A timeless emotion is within my soul,
The future so distant, as the memories grow.
For all that I have is in my mind,
And, no searching journey shall help me find.
Where are you now, are you too all alone,
Do you stand like a stranger,
To what you have known?

my love

My love for you, has no bounds
For it surpasses the furthest star,
And like the sunlight coming down
It shall shine upon where you are.

take flight

Take flight to your dreams,
Leave the past behind.
Soar above the clouds,
A destiny you will find.

for joanna

If friendship is a journey,
I shall walk until the end.
Recalling all the memories,
And to the future I would tend.
For like a summer garden,
How like the flowers you are.
Full of life and colour,
And always never far.
For through the years of travelling,
You were there, when I tried to hide.
And I pray when you too were lonely,
You felt me by your side.

the gift

I can see the future in your eyes.
I can hear the laughter you
Have gifted our child.
So precious a gift, only
You could bestow.
For you touch our hearts,
You hold our dreams,
And I shall walk with you always,
As you place your hand in mine
And make us one.

always

Timeless are the moments with you,
Held tenderly in the hands of time.
Together as we always knew,
When you gave your heart to mine.

still in love

I will still love you, when
My pen can no longer write.
I shall remember always
As I watch day rest upon night.
And as I wonder at the gloaming,
That precious silent hour.
I know that you are beside me,
As your love around me towers.

I remember you

The memories of you, shall
Always remain within me.
Like a child caught in time,
Playing by the edge of the sea.

she sits alone

She sits alone, I know, though not there.
I see her dreams, held close with care.
The memories help her fall asleep.
Enclosed in words, her mind does keep.

Like a secret garden, walled in with pride.
A hidden door, so she can hide,
Among the flowers, that bloom each day.
But knowing, here she cannot stay.

It is only, just to sit a while,
And hear the echoes to bring a smile.
Do not sit alone, hear the future cry.
For I can see the memories, in your eyes.

And if you dare, to give a key.
I would sit and wait for you to see.
Like you, I have a place to belong,
Holding your hand forever, to hear your song.

flightless

Like a useless feather, I fall from your heart.
Once belonging to you, now flightless, falling apart.
Only a changeable wind can help me take flight,
With no directional meaning, you are no longer in sight.
So now I lie upon an honest distant shore,
No more soaring above the ocean, to the one I adore.

close

In my mind you are always near,
Just a touch away to calm my fears.

you

You are,
Therefore I am.
You cease
The winds,
And bring
The calm.

forest thoughts

timeless laughter

I am sure I hear your laughter,
When I walk amongst the trees.
A wooded land of memories,
Surrounds with reassuring ease.
The forest floor is carpeted
With bells of painted blue,
And when I kneel to touch them,
The bells ring out for you.

I stand beside the waters edge,
Reflecting the beauty of this place.
But when I look inside I
See your smiling face.
The wind swirls all around me
With a message soft and dear,
For I can hear your laughter,
As the echoes bring you near.

I reply with just a whisper as it
Ripples down the lake,
And I watch you place it in a pocket
Of special, rare keepsakes.
You may have, so long ago
Left me all alone,
But a promise, to your laughter
Is the seed that you have sown.

untitled

I return to bluebell wood,
But only in my mind.
For long years have passed now,
And the pathways slowly wind.

But I know within my heart,
I would find you standing there,
As if you waited all my life,
In case I returned to share.

my future is in the water,
Reflected by times relentless hand.
Looking to see you behind me,
Where you always stand.

For no matter if the bluebells,
Have had their short-lived flower.
I can walk towards them always,
As they call the coming hours.

So when I need to reach you,
I hear those calling bells.
And return to show my life to you,
The way only I can tell.

I shall meet you by the water,
Beside the mirrored lake.
And share my hopes and promises,
For you to proudly take.

alone

A sunlit path leads me
Slowly through the trees,
Guiding me towards a forest,
Full of memories.
I look up towards sunlight
As it shines upon the ground,
And step into the warmth
Of the love I have found.
For I have walked out of
The shadows even though, they are
Still there.
But I am no longer alone,
With the love I have to share.

the oak tree

I remember you,
As I know I should.
Standing in the
Meadows, where the
Oak tree stood.

Underneath, resting
In the shade.
My heart never left,
The memory stayed.

The silent leaves, fell
To the ground.
Like autumn snowflakes,
Falling all around.

Swaying branches, laid
Bare to the wind,
A thoughtful breeze,
Echoed from within.

I remember you,
For you grew like the trees.
Centuries of love, tender
Like falling leaves.

forgotten dreams

Forgotten are the dreams that
Lie upon the mist,
Swathed and cloaked in a
Shroud of darkness.
But remembered are the promises,
The sunlight tried to kiss,
Through a winter wood, leaf less
In it's starkness.

the flowers

The flowers turn,
When you walk by.
A breathless wind,
Lets out a sigh.
The path you walk,
Can never stay.
For all around changes,
When you walk away.

bluebell wood

I walk among the bells of blue,
That ring out the passing hours.
How many times have they called out,
As the woodland around me towers.

A darkness falls on the shadowed ground,
As nightfall quickens the pace.
For the night can hear those calling bells
Entering twilight, with a dancers grace.

forest thoughts

one

Through the darkest forest,
Beyond the centuries of trees.
I walk to find my future and
Mislay my memories.
For they ache so deep inside me,
And weigh upon my heart,
And now I must release them,
So these deep emotions part.

two

I listen, as the wind blows,
Carrying the falling leaves
Down upon the forest floor,
As they nestle beneath the trees.

three

The mist in the early morning, lies
Just above the forest floor.
Like the clouds in a tempest sky,
When the rain begins to pour.
And through this milky haze swirled
Lightly by the breeze,
I see a woodland full of promises
That grow among the trees.

four

Shall I stray from the path
Or journey forward to the unknown
Guided by a pathway of dreams,
A tree lined destiny that
Grows with each step?

five

Walk into the forest.
Listen to the silence
That lingers within the mist.
Look upon the beauty
Dawning, a new
Day, yet to be kissed.

seasons of change

the eve of christmas

The winter wind blows, the soft falling snow
Across a peaceful hallowed land.
A whispering song, lamenting and strong
Takes our memories by the hand.
On a journey so far, to the brightest star
That has guided so many through the years.
For tonight is the time, when all the stars align
A path to follow beyond all our fears.
For it is christmas eve, a time to receive
Peace akin to a silent starlit night.
Hear an angel's prayer, for those who we care,
As it falls softly with the snowflakes of white.

the storm

Be gone, my tormented heart.
Take flight to the angry black clouds of pain,
That roll in such agony across a thunderous
Incensed sky.
Let me only look upon this dark feeling of
Wretched torture.
For I can no longer, endure each daunting
Spasm of lightning, as it crackles through the
Static shadowy sky.

Let me not feel the rain fall hard upon
My shivering body,
If only I could wash a little of this startled
Confusion away.
So too, the sky breaks it heart, it might, just might,
Engulf my own frightened cries.
But alas, this heart weeps with such ferocity
Resounding in my head.
Only to be calmed by a nomadic wind that tells
An incessant tale, that I have heard too many times before.

So, reaching up to the sky, I use my hand to pen the
Conclusion, and once again I become the author of this
Tragic story.
Be gone, my suffering heart, be gone. Join the night
Watchman in the sky,
For I, no longer wish to be the keeper of this tempestuous,
Hopeless pain.

ode to winter

The autumn leaves fall through the breeze,
Leaving a carpet of the purest gold.
The landscape is bare, climbing the seasonal stair,
As winter waits to take its hold.
The fresh morning sun, reflecting rivers that run,
Through a forest of golden dreams.
This expectant land, now takes the hand,
Of winter, and guides it through this scene.
And when it lets go the soft falling snow,
Shall rest upon all in its sight.
The stars in the sky, the snowflakes that lie,
Sparkle together on this peaceful night.

tired darkness

I do not wish to walk alone,
And tread a path to the unknown.
I call the winds, so I take flight,
And rest me down away from sight.
So from the distance I can see
The future where I long to be,
But even if I called a storm,
No wind can take me from this harm.
So I stand awaiting fear, and watch
The shadows slowly appear.

The darkness creeps slowly down the walls,
No one hears my stifled calls.
For all alone I watch my fate.
I locked the doors, and shut the gate.
For who would want to hear my pleas,
And see me falling to my knees.
No, I keep this pain locked up inside,
Far better now, for me to hide.

camomile lawn

For who will lay beside me
On the camomile lawn,
And sense the coming summer,
And feel that winter has gone?
So if I think of seasons,
You are behind winter's door,
Not willing to unlock it
And see how I adore.

you bring the sunshine

You bring the sunshine,
You are a summer breeze.
A peaceful wave,
Leaving a lamenting sea.

You bring the sunshine
To every day.
Not a single cloud,
Now you are here to stay.

You bring the sunshine,
On the darkest of nights.
As you become the moon,
And keep the light.

You bring the sunshine,
To my heart.
Everyday is summer,
When the morning starts.

morning rain

The rain falls through a
Blanket of grey sky.
The hills on the horizon
Touch the clouds that cry.

castle

Held in a moment of time
Suspended by the surrounding mist.

goodbye my love

What is love, if I am without your grace.
Feeling helpless, in an empty place?

No walls to enclose my rising pain,
Just a vast, empty life, of the same.

Each sunrise, counts the many days,
Without a love, I lose my way.

A knowing moon, brings in the night.
Bidding farewell to the sun, setting out of sight.

Just as you bid farewell, to my love,
My heart left to fall, like the sun up above.

But, the sun and moon cannot share the sky,
So I shall take my place, and watch the days go by.

Goodbye my love, I shall see you at twilight,
A passing glance as, I set out of sight.

ode to summer

The once bare winter trees,
Now cloaked in a vision of green.
Draped in an emerald vision,
As the branches become unseen.

For summer is patiently waiting,
Upon the seasonal stair.
And paints the land with colour,
Brushing away the bare.

The life that was, once hidden,
Behind a blanket of rain.
Has risen back to life, and
Blossomed once again.

And as the scent of flowers,
Tempts the summer breeze.
It rises to the sky, and
Nestles between the trees.

chasing pain

I run into the darkness
To lose this chasing pain.
But as my footsteps quicken,
The fear around me gains.
It joins the falling teardrops,
And drenches my tired soul,
Then rises up beyond my breath,
And slowly takes its hold.

I stumble through the evening
Shade, and reach out my shaking hands.
For a coldness has taken over,
And wrapped around me where I stand.

I sit under the full moon, a spotlight
To guide my way.
But I shall sit here, solitude, over and over
Night becoming day.

exchanging time

If forever is with you, it shall come too soon.
How many sunrises, and not enough moons?
Too many tides that rise to the shores,
They count the days, each sooner than before.
The sands of time, stretch out on the beach.
For all those grains, seconds out of my reach.
And all the seasons give time to the days,
Stop the autumn and winter, keep the sunrays.
But I know it is hopeless, time shall take its hold.
Exchanging time for eternity, so we never grow old.

20th century vox

Who will start to listen when the sun begins to fade,
Leaving us in silence in an unfamiliar shade?

Who will mend the flowers, when no longer they can bloom,
To bequeath the earth to echo a long forgotten tomb?

Who will watch the tide come in with polluted blackened fear,
As the oceans are made of water of so many salted tears?

Who will say they are sorry for what was said and done,
And sail away unwritten words spoken by everyone?

Who will look around them and use their seeing eyes,
And listen with their deafened ears, and hear the haunting cries?

Who will walk ahead of us, even though the road is unpaved,
And stop our history repeating the way we have behaved?

Who will stand alone amongst a graveyard of fallen trees,
Remembering a time gone by as they crumple to their knees?

Who will touch the earth, and feel the weeping scars,
And realise we are existing on a fragile precious star?

Who will take a deep breath and blow away the sunless clouds,
So we can live in harmony and remove our deathly shrouds?

daybreak

A scented summer morning,
Awakens a new day.
Walking in the sunlight,
As the world around you plays.

sunlit dreams

What are words if they
Cannot tell of my love.
Cutting them out and
Placing them as stars above.
Making them float
On silver streams,
Letting the river glisten
With sunlit dreams.
They shall hush the wind,
And silence the song.
So my undying words
Can rest upon.

the loch

I stood on the mountain,
I took flight to the skies.
I sailed on the loch,
Reflecting my sighs.
I stood at the edge,
Felt the wind take its place.
Chasing the future,
To catch it with grace.

I walked the path,
I followed my lead.
I saw the horizon,
And took heed.
To return to my past,
A defiant cry.
Keeping my journey inside,
As fate walks by.

I looked upon the
Heather, bracken and ferns.
In awe of their beauty,
Across the hills that yearn.
Stretched out all around me,
A formidable sight.
Desperate to remember,
Before the fading light.

Knowing where I belong,
I can recall with such ease.
The colour of the heather,
The surrounding trees.
This place has such,
A breathless, silent way.
Silence, the only sound,
Day after day.

christmas poems

one

An angels wings around me,
As the choirs echoes true.
A peaceful time at Christmas,
Like the love I found in you.

two

Guided by the stars as they
Take their place upon this eve.
Looking towards a Christmas heaven,
You and I as we always believed.

three

Echoes from the church walls,
On this silent night.
Carried on the airs breath,
Surrounded by candle light.

four

May you walk upon the pure fresh snow,
Like an angel in the night.
Leaving a path of footprints, is all
That is left in sight.

five

Honest as a snowflake.
True as the candlelight.
Angelic as the carols.
Silent as this night.

six

My gift to you,
To hear laughter
each day.
And to receive
Your love,
In the words,
You say.

seven

I know I walked with an angel,
When you held my dreams on high,
And took your place beside them,
In a starlit heavenly sky.

eight

The stars seem brighter,
On this peaceful night.
Guiding me home for
Christmas, like candlelight.

nine

Ring out the bells
Light every tree.
Let the snow fall
Honest and free.

Hear the echoes
Arise the choir.
Fill the night with song
To the highest spire.

Place a star on top
Of each tree.
To guide every heart
On christmas eve.

ten

Our tree stands,
Like no other.
Resplendent,
By our past.
Decorated with all
Our memories.
Adorned with love
To last.

distant echoes

one

Distant are the echoes, that
Once brought you near.
How am I to follow
When no longer I can hear.
Who shall I now turn to,
So I can share my love.
How can I continue,
My pain has had enough.

two

You held my hand in the darkness,
Even though there were no pleas.
You walked along beside me,
When I fell upon my knees.
You talk to me so softly, even through
The pouring rain.
You kept me above the water,
And washed away my pain.

three

When I close my eyes you are there.
Holding the emotions I have laid bare.

four

I still dream of you
For that is all I have.
For the warm nights,
Replaced by lonely hours.
You are gone, so you share
My dreams.
Like you once did through
My waking days.

five

I turn to tell you stories,
But forget that you were not there.
I glanced to see you smiling,
The reflection was left bare.
I listened for your footsteps,
But the echoes have no hold.
The silence left me numb,
Even though I had been told.

six

Through a mist of memories
You walk into my sight.
Clouded by the future
Given only one last rite.
For you can no longer journey,
Empty is that place.
Only in a cherished memory
Is where you forever grace.

animal prints

one

I shall never tire of walking
To make my journeys end,
Reaching out across the
Miles, to feel the love I send.

two

Resting in the shadows,
I feel the cooling breeze.
Sheltered from the sunlight
Beneath the shading trees.

three

Destined by surroundings,
Through the night and day
Sleeping under a sunset.
Awake in the moons foray.

four

Listen as the wind blows
Across the stark terrain,
Waiting for the clouds to
Come and bring the cooling rain.

five

A sleepless night is calling
As the land begins to wake.

six

Solitude by choice,
Surrounded by the peace.
A day of distant yearnings,
As the noise begins to cease.

seven

What beauty lies before me,
And rises in the haze.
Lit up by a bright new sun,
That lasts throughout the day.

stargazing

one

I kissed goodbye tomorrow,
And held on to the past.
I ran towards the sunset,
And saw my shadow cast.
I waited for the moonrise,
So I could count the stars,
And place you all among them,
So you are never far.

two

On a night without clouds
The sky forever lasts.
For heaven has removed its shroud,
Letting the moon slowly past.
For no matter where I travel
The stars remain the same.
And as my fate unravels,
I shall follow those tiny flames.

three

When I look up to the night sky
I can walk amongst the stars.

four

If you were the moon, then bring daylight to night.
If you were the horizon, I would sail into sight.
If you were the stars, I would journey from the shore.
If you were the sun, then let it shine forever more.

held in time

you smiled

You were a guiding angel,
By my side.
You held me close,
When I tried to hide.
You smiled, and so did all
Who looked upon,
For they saw your beauty,
Like the morning dawn.
Your love came from your
Heart, so kind,
Never losing sight of life's
Hands of time.
But that stopped, when you
Silently took your leave.
Giving too much time for
Me to grieve.

in my heart

For without you, I no
Longer have your touch.
But in every day and night,
I love you as much.
As if you were holding
My hand,
And by my side you shall
Always stand.
For you left your love,
And you gave your heart.
So I am never alone,
And we shall never part.

I was there

I saw you by the ocean and,
Heard the tears you cried.
I wish you could have felt
My love upon the rising tide.
But all alone, you stood there,
Wiping away the tears.
I sent all my heart, to carry
Away your rising fears.
So when you return to the ocean,
Leave your pain behind.
For I am there, beside the shore,
Inside your heart and mind.

waiting for you

Do not tread a lonely path,
As winter takes its hold.
But walk under a summer sun,
Among the fields of gold.
For standing there beside you,
I wait to take your hand,
Waiting, silently, beyond your fate,
To help you understand.
When you remember me, see only
My smiling face.
And there, inside your kindest
Heart, I shall always grace.
For I too, wish to hear your laughter,
As I wait for you.
Knowing one day, we shall walk again,
Upon the morning dew.

sun through my window

Sun through my window,
Shines upon the pain.
My eyes slowly close,
As sleep tries in vain.
To dream of you, would
Bring you near.
More memories, to keep
And far less tears.
But the sun goes on shining,
And I must take heart.
And look upon each morning,
As the pain begins to start.
Sun shines through my window,
I shall sit, and enjoy the warm.
And feel you coming closer,
Keeping my dreams from harm.

stolen dreams

How can I still love you, when
You came and stole the dreams,
That were part of my being, and
Kept, my thoughts unseen?
Searching, long now, but it is
Not my mind,
That looks within, and cannot find.
It is the heart, that is restless
And confused.
Broken, shattered, left behind
And used.
I shall stop loving you, set
Adrift downstream.
How could I still love you,
The one who stole my dreams.

where are the promises?

Where are the promises, you once gave,
When I fought alone, the world I braved.
I honoured your love, and placed it beyond,
So I could walk onwards, to where I belonged.
But, the promises like a rainbow faded after the rain,
And I watched the mist take over, and the clouds regain.
Where are you now, with those silent words,
Meaningless promises that took flight with the birds?
I shall now paint my own, honest blue skies,
And fill them with my dreams upon sacred wings to fly.

maybe if?

Maybe if I had shared with you,
Like I did the listening sea,
All the pain that was rising,
And the confusion within me.

Maybe if I had held you, longer
And kissed you in a way,
That would have spoken the
Timid words, my heart could not say.

Maybe if I had waited, and
Turned to see your face.
I would have seen pain in your eyes,
I had put in place.

Maybe if I had listened, I would
Have heard your silent pain,
And recognised myself in you,
And seen the coming rain.

Maybe if the clouds clear, and
The mist begins to rise,
I will see you once again, and
Silence the lonely cries.

baby bluebells

learning to fly

A tiny little faerie was learning to fly,
All she wanted to do was reach to the sky.
Hopping and jumping with all of her might,
But try as she did, she couldn't take flight.

She stamped her feet, and kicked the leaves,
She tutted at birds, stuck her tongue out at bees.
Flying by they showed their disgust, saying
'A flightless faerie you are, we trust"
'Why am I so stupid, when you can use your wings"
Being left out, really wasn't her thing.

But just when she felt, she had had enough,
And made her way, stomping in a faerie huff.
A flutter of wings echoed from beyond.
A vision appeared for what she so longed.
Hundreds of faeries flying to be by her side,
Stretching out their tiny hands to be her guide.

Without a glance, her feet left the ground,
For faerie dust was all around.
It sparkled and glistened like little fire flies,
And before she knew it she had touched the sky.

which witch?

Does a witch, like to stitch,
Or send clothes to the tailor's?
And would she, sail on the sea,
Or leave that job to sailors?

And in a class, would she pass,
All the hard exams?
Maybe she'd sit, and use her wit
Changing everyone to frogs – hizzamm!!

Is her cat, black and fat,
Or is he ginger and stripy?
For a proper witch, that would be a hitch,
So I don't think that's too likely.

One thing she's got, is a cooking pot,
And an old leather book of spells.
What ever she makes, it certainly not cakes.
You know by the horrible smells.

So which is witch, and can she switch,
Spells when it takes her notion.
So if a witch, knew which was which,
Oh! Whatever! Let her get on with making potions.

nutty!!

There once was a squirrel who did like to hurl,
Nuts at passers by.
He'd aim out of sight, with all of his might,
So it looked like they came from the sky.
With a cheeky wee wiggle, and a squirrel's giggle,
He threw them all day long.
Until one day, unfortunate, shall we say,
He got one back on his head like a gong!

bumbley bees

Bumbley bees have knobbly knees,
They jump up and down on flowers.
They do it all day in the sunrays,
They just do it for hours and hours.
With a busy hum hum and a sting in their bum,
They fly from stem to stem.
Then once they are fed they go to their beds,
And wake up, to do it all over again.

mr fox

Mr fox wears red socks,
To keep him nice and cosy.
And if you pass, and dare to ask,
He says "don't you be so nosy".

For every morn, he does adorn,
His socks of splendid red.
Up to his knees, with the greatest of ease,
Until its time for bed.

So no matter the day, you will hear him say,
"where are my socks of crimson?"
For he knows when, he wiggles his toes,
He loves the socks, he lives in.

So if you see a fox that wears red socks,
And you stop to take a peek,
He is off to try, and find socks to buy,
So he has a pair for each day of the week.

charming farming

There was a cow, who liked to row,
With anyone who would listen.
It sounded rude, when she moo'd,
So she sniffed her nose that glistened.

A little pig, who wore a wig,
And made all the farmyard laugh.
He kept it on, and sang a song,
Even when he took a bath.

And there was sam, a little lamb,
Who thought he was so cool.
But everyone spotted, when he trotted,
He was made of cuddly wuddly wool.

But of course, there was a horse,
Who walk, trotted, and cantered.
He was never late with these three gaits,
Together with his jovial banter.

There was a bull, and he did rule,
All his farmyard mates.
But if you find you are absent of mind
Don't forget to shut the gate!!

Then when it's dark, farmer clark,
Puts all the animals to bed.
He turns out the light, so they're out of sight,
And walks away shaking his head.

It must be charming to do your farming,
With a bunch of farmyard friends.
But as he said its time for bed,
And this day must come to an end.

commotion in the ocean

Does a crab, hail a cab,
Or does he take the train?
And does he tip, or give a nip,
When he boards a plane?

Does a shell, like to tell
Stories to passers by?
And do their tales, interest whales,
Or do they have bigger fish to fry?

Does a seal, like to peel,
Oranges with their flippers?
Or is that silly, cos its far too chilly,
They're too busy wearing slippers?

Do the penguins, enjoy sending,
Letters by first class post?
Or do they do flips, when they take dips,
The thing they like the most?

Do blue whales, chase their tails,
Using their mighty fins?
And do they get dizzy, making the water fizzy,
Going round and round in a spin?

Do the squids, like to get rid,
Of their jets of ink?
Or are their wishes, just to wash dishes,
In the kitchen sink?

Do the sharks, like to remark,
On how their teeth are sparkling clean?
Is it because they know, and just like to show?
They are the biggest you have ever seen.?!

Does a sting ray, spend all day,
On the ocean bed in the sand?
Or would he like, to ride a bike,
To the music of a marching band?

Does a mermaid use a spade,
To dig her underwater garden?
And can she hear, under all that hair,
Or says "you what, I beg your pardon."

Does an octopus, get very cross,
When his legs get in a tangle,
But he's tied bells, so he can tell,
Which is which if they dingle or dangle?

Does a dolphin like to golf in,
Plus fours made of bright red tartan.
But they have fins, so where would you begin,
You would be finished before you were starting?

Does neptune, love to play a tune,
On his long grey whiskers?
Along with the carps on their harps,
A seaside session, until they get blisters.

Do I wish I could swim like a fish,
And see the creatures of the ocean?
It could be done, and would be fun,
To part of all that silly commotion!!

bungle in the jungle (a hungry tale)

There are odd things
Being dished in the jungle.
Like green beans,
Served with apple crumble.
But you have to be nice,
When offered a slice.
For to say no would
Be a jungle bungle.

An elephant called ellie
Ate lots of wibbely wobbly jelly.
She'd stick her trunk in,
And give it a spin,
So it ended up in her belly!

Nowhere is safe for carrots!
For they are hunted down by parrots.
They swoop from the trees,
In great colourful ease.
In formation like fighter pilots.

A crocodile called snappy,
Did the one thing that made him happy.
He would sit in his lake,
And eat chocolate cake.
Which made snappy a happy chappy!

A hungry tiger called brian,
Got ravenous at all he spied on.
Which made his friends aware,
When he started to stare,
A friend for dinner; he had his eye on!

A hungry monkey called pete.
Filled his cheeky wee face
With sweets.
The only bananas,
Were on his pyjamas.
Something he never ever
Wanted to eat.

A very large python
Called jake.
Had an unusual craving
For a snake.
He liked broccoli and cheese,
With big juicy peas.
And a side order of
Blueberry cake.

George, the long
Necked giraffe.
When he ate, made
The animals laugh.
He loved honey on bread,
And with a flick of his head.
It went down his long neck
Like a path.

Lucas, the very cool lizard.
Made food appear
Like a magical wizard.
He ate so fast,
When his food went past.
He was surrounded in
A lunch like blizzard.

Emma, the little gazelle,
Liked to crunch
Her apples well.
With the utmost of style,
She would flash her big smile.
Saying "they're good for
Your teeth, can't you tell?"

Jordan, the jungle king.
A lion who did
Like to sing.
"Give me chocolate all day,
Ice cream come what may,
Ah! food.....such a
Wonderful thing!!"

Well, the jungle is a very
Strange place.
And if you ever,
Happen to grace.
You know you're a winner
When invited to dinner.
Just make sure to leave
Enough space.

index of first lines